HE IS RISEN!

This gift is for

Rita Avila

From

Steve & Family

MICHAEL CARD

IMMANUEL

THOUGHTS ON
THE LIFE OF CHRIST

THOMAS NELSON PUBLISHERS
Nashville

Loneliness

Published in Nashville, Tennessee, by Thomas Nelson, Inc., and distributed in Canada by Lawson Falle, Ltd., Cambridge, Ontario.

**Library of Congress
Cataloging-in-Publication Data**

Card, Michael. 1957-
    Immanuel : thoughts on the life of Christ / by Michael Card.
        p.   cm.
    ISBN 0-8407-7809-0
    1. Jesus Christ—Biography—Meditations. I. Title.
BT306.4.C37 1993
232.9'01—dc20   92-37893
                                                                CIP

Printed in Singapore.
1 2 3 4 5 — 96 95 94 93

In Him was life, and the life was
the light of men.

The
Final Word

*And so the Light became alive
And manna became Man.
Eternity came into time
So we could understand.*

Behind all the negative voices trying to stop me from writing this book is one single, gentle Voice that says, "I believe you can do it."

Finding the right words for a lyric doesn't seem as difficult to me as filling a page with prose.

All our words are only stuttering and stammering in comparison to that one final, perfect Word, the Word of God.

To say that Jesus is the Word is another way of saying He is God speaking to us.

By the Word, Light became a living being. Manna became man. Wisdom became a person. In Him, Life came to life; all that God is came to us in that One Final Word we call Jesus. My struggle to find words to describe Jesus is at the same time a struggle to find Him.

The Promise

The Promise was love.
And the Promise was life.
The Promise meant light to the
world.
Living proof "Jehovah saves,"
For the name of the Promise
was Jesus.

A long time ago I made a special promise to someone. I ended up breaking that promise.

I felt less a person after I broke that promise. I learned from that experience that when you make a real promise, a little bit of yourself goes along with it.

Our God is the great maker of
promises. His Word, the Bible, is
quite simply a collection of the
promises He has made to us.

Through these promises, God was trying to give something of Himself to Adam, to Israel—and to us. The Bible tells us that when the Promised One, Jesus, finally came, the Lord poured all of Himself into Him. In the fullness of time what God had desired to do through the ages happened: He gave all of Himself to us through Jesus Christ, the Word of God, spoken at an incalculable price.

Immanuel

*I*mmanuel.
Our God is with us.
And if God is with us,
Who could stand against us?
Our God is with us.
Immanuel.

We got married in December. Susan, my bride-to-be, had just finished finals, that day in fact. In the nervousness, I forgot much of what was said and done around us.

I do clearly remember the homily, however. Our pastor, my dear friend, spoke a word of great power and promise. The word was *Immanuel*: "God with us."

*I*mmanuel was a wonderful word to hear. For it means Jesus is with us every moment of every hour of every day of our lives.

The apostle Paul realized the indescribable gift of Immanuel in a passage which many consider the height of his inspiration. He concludes, "If God is for us, who could be against us?"

"Never will I leave you, never will I forsake you," Jesus says. That is what our pastor was trying to tell us on that first day of our life together. Immanuel. God is with you, now and forever.

Celebrate the Child

Celebrate the Child who is the
Light.
Now the darkness is over.
No more wandering in the night.
Celebrate the Child who is the
Light.

Christmas is a struggle for my wife and me. Our ongoing war with the world seems to intensify as the decorations go up all over town.

If Christianity could just be
seen for what it is—a paradox
and a mystery.

The beginning in that dirty stable is one of the greatest mysteries: the plainness and the greatness of Jesus, the grime and the glory. The birth of a gentle Lamb who was the fiercest Lion.

If Christmas means anything to you, then it must mean everything.

Celebrate? you say. Yes, most heartily, amidst the dung of the stable, which is, of course, the ruse of the world.

Celebrate at the foot of that ghastly cross because it is the hope of the world. Gather around a cattle trough and celebrate a baby born in poverty and rejected because He is the Savior of the world!

Now That I've Held Him in My Arms

Simeon takes the boy and starts to
sing.
"Now that I've held Him in my
arms
My life can come to an end."

"*L*et Your servant now depart in peace.
I've seen Your salvation.
He's the Light of the Gentiles,
And the glory of His people Israel."

Simeon was an old man when
he received a very special
promise from God. The promise?
You will not die until you have
seen the coming of the Messiah.

It was good news to finally be able to embrace the Promised One. But the best news of all is that He embraces us.

The reason for Simeon's song?
Deep inside his tired old heart,
he knew that the infant he held
in his arms was in truth the One
who had been holding him all
his life long.

The Voice of the Child

Come listen awhile to the voice of
the Child.
Stand in awe of the Wisdom of
God.
Hear what He has to say,
For the time is today.
You can come or just walk away.

I am an old rabbi.
Where's the Child who was here
only yesterday?
How my heart started to beat as I
sat at His feet!
Oh, the things He'd say.
I've just got to find Him and tell
Him I'm sorry
I walked away.

In the face of a lack of detail of Jesus's childhood we are left to our own imaginations to take our place alongside the teachers and listen to that small voice speak as no one had ever spoken before.

I've always imagined an elderly rabbi who was just curious enough to stay for awhile and listen to the young Jesus.

I suppose the rabbi of my imagination is really me. I would have stood and listened only as long as my schedule allowed. I pray that, like the rabbi, I would have come back to find that little boy who spoke the words of God.

The Baptism

He came gently and stepped down
into the water;
With the light of the Father in His
face.
Son of God He had been since the
beginning.
Now as Son of Man Jesus took His
place.

Baptism is literally a washing. It is symbolically a death, burial, and resurrection.

Submitting to baptism is a sign
of a repentant heart. For such a
simple act it can be seen to have
many meanings.

Something we have forgotten amidst our debate on the meaning of baptism is that baptism is truly a mystery.

Jesus obeyed God and was baptized. From his obedience—an obedience that submits to what may seem senseless, that does not demand to see the meaning of it all—from that kind of obedience came the salvation of the world.

The Wedding

Lord of Light,
Please come to this wedding.
Take the doubt and darkness away.
Turn the water of lifeless living
To the wine of gladness, we pray.

So amidst the laughter and
feasting,
There sits Jesus, full with the fun!
He has made them wine
Because He is longing
For a wedding that's yet to come.

W herever and whenever Christians come together, parties should break out because we follow a Savior who is preoccupied with them. Whenever Jesus wasn't preaching or teaching you'd find Him at a party.

It was at a party that Jesus performed His first miracle. The miracle was the turning of the water into wine, some four hundred gallons of it!

The concept of the party was important not only to Jesus but to the early church as well. The fellowship of the early Christians was a primary source of evangelism in those first days of the faith.

If Jesus seemed to be particularly excited about the wedding feast in Cana, I believe it was because He was looking ahead to that final feast, where He, the Bridegroom, will finally be brought together with us, His Bride.

Loneliness

*In Gethsemane You needed
someone near; . . .
Just to have somebody close to You,
Even if they were asleep,
Even though they never seemed to
understand.*

That you walk in lonely places.
You fill the empty spaces
That living in a lonely world can
cause.
And knowing that You're with me
now,
And knowing that You care
somehow,
Makes my loneliness just draw me
close to You.

I have always struggled with loneliness. It's not because I don't have a wonderful family and friends. Sometimes it's precisely because they are so special and so numerous that I feel that way.

Someone once described
loneliness as being ill at ease
with the world but at peace with
the universe.

At those lonely times I often think about Jesus. It's no surprise that all four Gospels talk about His loneliness and the preference for "lonely places."

When Jesus felt alone, it was because His Father was so visibly absent in the world. Jesus sought His presence in lonely places. I wonder if their hearts resonated together with loneliness . . . for each other.

Every time we let loneliness
take over our feelings, we have
lost sight of that personal,
caring, and loving Father. Even if
no other person understands or
cares, He does. That is the God
Jesus fled to when He felt lonely.

Light of the World

You are the Light of the World,
Oh, Lord,
And You make Your servants shine.
So how could there be any darkness
in me
If You are the Light of the World?

Wipe every tear away, Oh, Lord,
And teach us the song of the Lamb.
Your promise is true but it's still up
to You
To wipe every tear away.

Come to the Table

Come to the table.
He's prepared for you
The bread of forgiveness, the wine
of release.
Come to the table and sit down
beside Him.
The Savior wants you to join in the
feast.

I can remember the exact spot where I sat one Sunday morning while I was still in college. No one in church was prepared for what the Lord was about to do. How do you prepare yourself for an encounter with God?

Our pastor began talking about sin. Quite unexpectedly, he began to list particular sins. The feeling of guilt and conviction was heavy in the air.

At the very moment when we all thought the pastor was going to push us into the pit we had all dug for ourselves, he threw us a rope. The table of the Lord. It was for us.

The table was for all of us. The bread and the cup. His body. "For I did not come to judge the world, but to save it," Jesus said. His words really were true.

For the first time in my life communion became "Holy Communion." Communion now meant life and peace and joy.

Jesus welcomes you and me as
His special guests to the
communion table, to be
astounded at His generosity.

Cross of Glory

U*pon the cross of glory,*
His death was life to me,
A sacrifice of love's most sacred
mystery.
And death rejoiced to hold Him,
Though soon He would be free.
For love must always have the
victory.

The crucifix can be found on the communion table, on the lapel of a businessman, hanging from the ear of a heavy metal singer, and in the corner of a business card. I'm not so sure what the cross means in all of these places.

There is a movement to empty the cross of its meaning. The cross used to stand for Jesus, more precisely, the suffering of Jesus. Now it stands for an institution that most often doesn't really stand for anything.

The early Christians had other symbols for Jesus, the fish or icthus.

Why didn't they utilize the symbol of the cross? My guess is that they shied away from representing the cross because it meant too much, not because it meant too little.

The cross is not a symbol. It is the center of the universe, the nexus of history, the most meaningful event that ever took place. Though the world, both pagan and Christian, seems bent on reducing the meaning of the cross, it is irreducible.

Love Crucified Arose

Love crucified arose.
The risen One in splendor;
Jehovah's soul defender;
Has won the victory.
Love crucified arose.
And the grave became a place of
hope,
For the heart that sin and sorrow
broke
Is beating once again.

When I was young, whenever I looked at a deceased body, one thought kept repeating itself: There is no way in the world this person is ever going to get up again! Yet Jesus Christ did just that. He rose from the dead!

The details of the resurrection seem to point to the fact that there was an absence of haste. Jesus took the time to unwrap the cloth from around His face and fold it up.

The fact of Jesus' resurrection is the reason for our hope that we will rise again as well.

I wonder if there will be the same absence of haste when my own eyes, through dust and ashes, slowly open to finally see His face.

El Shaddai

El Shaddai, El Shaddai, El Elyon
na Adonai,
Age to age You're still the same,
By the power of the name.
El Shaddai, El Shaddai, Erekamka
na Adonai,
We will praise and lift You high
El Shaddai.

Though God is One He is known in the Old Testament by many names. This song attempts to present the paradox of Jesus by focusing on a few of these names.

El means "God." Shaddai means "strong" or "mighty." God first revealed Himself as El Shaddai to Abram when he confirmed the covenant with him.

El Elyon means "God Most High," or the God who is above all other gods.

Through His various names and acts of power, the Lord revealed Himself to the people of the Old Testament, and by those names He still reveals Himself to us today. When Jesus, the Son of God, appears, power is not the focus even though He does display His power in many ways.

Though God had spoken the universe into existence and displayed His power to the children of Israel, the most awesome triumph of El Shaddai was made possible only through the frailty of His only son.

Jesus died for you and me. By God's power He rose again, but we must never forget that first He died.

Joy in the Journey

There is a joy in the journey.
There's a light we can love on the
way.
There is a wonder and wildness to
life,
And freedom for those who obey.

The first Easter was probably an ordinary day. Jesus chose an ordinary day to transform the world and give us the chance to know joy.

Joy is hard to find on ordinary days, in the routine of daily life. On those mystical occasions when joy comes to us from beyond, the ordinary is transformed into a vehicle for true joy.

Jesus saves us not only from our sin and ourselves. He also saves us from our ordinariness. He transforms the drudgery of daily existence into a wonderful journey with Him.

Jesus gives us the secret to both
love and complete joy:
obedience.

There is a joy in our journey. It comes from obedience. It comes from beyond. It comes in spite of the ordinary, or perhaps because of it. It is another word for love, which is another word for Jesus.

Jesus, Let us Come to Know You

Jesus, let us
Come to know You.
Let us see You.
Face to face.
Touch us, hold us,
Use us, mold us,
Only let us
Live in You.